ANNIE SLOAN

DECORATIVE
DECOUPAGE

ANNIE SLOAN

DECORATIVE
DECOUPAGE

A PRACTICAL GUIDE

Photography by Geoff Dann

THE READER'S DIGEST ASSOCIATION, INC.

Pleasantville, New York/Montreal

A Reader's Digest Book

Conceived, edited, and designed by
Collins & Brown Limited

Editor Colin Ziegler
Assistant Editor Claire Waite
Art Director Roger Bristow
Designer Steve Wooster
DTP Designer Claire Graham
Photographer Geoff Dann

1 3 5 7 9 8 6 4 2

Library of Congress Cataloging in Publication Data:

Sloan, Annie, 1949–
    [Decoupage]
    Annie Sloan decoupage : a practical guide / photography by Geoff
Dann.
        p.   cm.
    ISBN 0-7621-0011-7
    1. Decoupage.   I. Title.
TT870.S57   1997
745.54'6–dc21   97-22197

Printed in Portugal

Contents

———— ❧ ————

Introduction

ECOUPAGE IS THE ART of cutting out paper designs and applying them to decorative objects, furniture, and walls. It was established in 18th-century France and Italy and by the 19th century had become a popular hobby for Victorian ladies. Today the technique can be used to mimic the traditional style, or can take on many modern variations. At its most basic, decoupage involves cutting out a design, such as a flower, gluing it to a surface, then applying many layers of varnish. Each of these steps – cutting, gluing, and varnishing – requires great care so that the end result does not resemble a piece of paper glued down, but looks like a hand-painted, hand-drawn, or stenciled design. Your eye should focus not on the paper edge, or on bubbles or folds in the paper, but on the design itself.

The book begins with all the information you need to ensure a good base for making your decoupage projects, including the types of objects (see pp. 10–11) and backgrounds (see pp. 12–13) you can use, sources of decoupage motifs (see pp. 14–17),

Preparing Motifs

ABOVE You can use a sharp, pointed pair of scissors or a craft knife not only to cut with precision, but to cut imaginatively and thereby enhance your design (see pp. 26–29). Here, a small bunch of grapes was cut out of a larger grape design.

Staining and Coloring

RIGHT Use watercolors, watersoluble pencils, inks, and teabags to color and stain black and white prints (see pp. 30–35). This motif was given a three-dimensional quality using shellac and pigments.

Gluing

ABOVE You can also use glue creatively (see pp. 36–39). The flower stalk of this motif was bent to one side while the paper was wet with glue.

and how to prepare surfaces (see pp. 18–21). *The Basic Techniques* chapter follows, covering the entire decoupage process from the purely technical skills of sealing and cutting motifs (see pp. 26–29), gluing (see pp. 36–39), and varnishing (see pp. 40–42), to ways of embellishing motifs with stains, colors, and decorative varnishes.

Originally, black and white motifs colored with watercolor paints were used for decoupage. *Staining and Coloring* (see pp. 30–35) explains other methods of embellishing motifs, such as using inks and watersoluble pencils, as well as how to stain new white paper with tea to give it an aged appearance, painting in shadows and highlights using pigment, shellac, and water-base paints, and painting in the background of your motif to match the color of the object being decoupaged. More advanced methods of varnishing, such as coloring varnish with pigments, and using crackle varnish or scratched varnish techniques (see pp. 43–47) to embellish your motifs are also explained.

The rest of the book comprises seven techniques for applying decoupage, with step-by-step instructions and inspirational objects to admire and copy. First, *Traditional Decoupage* (see pp. 50–53) – familiar to many people because of Victorian scrap screens – is explained and extended to include collage and positioning designs accurately using tracing paper.

Traditional Decoupage

BELOW One traditional method of decoupage (see pp. 50–53) is to position pictures, or scraps as they were known in the 19th century, close together and overlapping, to create scrap scenes on pieces of furniture (usually screens). This tray was decorated in that style, with overlapping figures and landscapes.

Varnishing and Finishing

ABOVE The type of varnish you use (see pp. 40–47) can enhance the character of your design. Modern and traditional varnishes are used, as well as pigmented and scratched varnishes and aging techniques. Here, crackle varnish was used in places on this panel, resulting in subtle cracks, which are most obvious at the base.

Decoupage on Glass (see pp. 54–61) shows the basic technique involved in positioning an image behind glass, so that you view the motif through the glass of a window, bowl, or door panel for instance. You can use different types of background, such as crackle paint and metal leaf, as well as applying tissue paper to give a stained-glass effect.

Decoupage with Freehand Painting (see pp. 62–65) can give your motif a loosely textured background, such as a conventional landscape or the rippling water surrounding a fish. Motifs cut from translucent tissue paper can look more solid and three-dimensional when combined with paint.

Decoupage with Metal Leaf (see pp. 66–69) describes two different methods. In the first you use metal leaf as a background, to give richness to your work. In the second you apply metal leaf to a paper motif, which you then cut out, to create an effect reminiscent of traditional Asian lacquerwork.

The Print Room (see pp. 70–75) is an 18th-century British technique in which original prints and paper borders are used to decorate entire rooms. Printed paper swags, ribbons, or ropes unite the prints. This technique can easily be adapted to decorate smaller objects and pieces of furniture.

Decoupage on Glass

ABOVE *This technique involves positioning motifs behind glass (see pp. 54–61), which makes the decoupage look sharp and clear. Use pictures, silhouettes, or designs in tissue paper, as shown, to create stained-glass effects, with backdrops of paint, crackle paint, or metal leaf for added effect.*

Decoupage with Freehand Painting

ABOVE *Freehand painting (see pp. 62–65) gives an added dimension to decoupage. Here, black and white fish motifs were enhanced with hand-painted lines and dots to create a water effect.*

Decoupage with Metal Leaf

ABOVE *This technique involves either gluing motifs to a background of metal leaf, as shown on this candlestick, or cutting motifs out of paper decorated with metal leaf, to create an Asian look. You can use imitation gold, silver, or copper metal leaf (see pp. 66–69).*

The final two techniques use both plain and patterned papers, rather than images of flowers, people, and so on. *Making Your Own Designs* (see pp. 76–83) shows you how simple it is to create your own decoupage motifs. You can use stencils and silhouettes as templates or make cuts in folded paper for a repeating effect. Scissorwork, inspired by traditional cutouts from China, Central European countries, and America, forms the basis of much homemade decoupage.

Building Designs with Colored Papers (see pp. 84–87) shows you how to create pictures using several different papers at one time. You can compose a simple design using torn plain paper in a number of colors, or take inspiration from inlaid work in wood, marble, and even appliquéd quilts, to build up faux marquetry designs.

The book concludes with the *Decoupage Library* (see pp. 88–93), six pages of black and white designs, in a variety of styles, which you can photocopy, and enlarge, if necessary, to use as motifs for your own decoupage projects.

The techniques described in *Decoupage* should offer something for everyone and extend the range of traditional decoupage to include a wider variety of possibilities. I hope the book inspires you to decorate furniture and small objects of all kinds, as well as entire walls.

Building Designs with Colored Papers

ABOVE *With this technique you can make your own designs with more than one paper at a time. You can use torn shapes to make patterns or use patterned papers, in imitation of marquetry, as here, inlaid marble work, and quilt designs (see pp. 84–87).*

The Print Room

ABOVE *The print room combines prints with border frames, ribbons, swags, and chains (see pp. 70–75), usually on a wall. However, you can also use the decorative detailing to adorn wastebaskets, like this one, and other small objects.*

Making Your Own Designs

ABOVE *You can make your own designs using plain or store-bought patterned papers (see pp. 76–83). Use templates or cut symmetrical designs like the tree on the door panel shown here.*

Types of Objects

Y OU CAN APPLY decoupage to all kinds of shapes and surfaces – wood, glass, plastic, and metal – although it is best to begin on flat objects before tackling curves or corners. The type and quality of your surface will determine which method of preparation you will need to follow before you can begin to decoupage. Old objects generally need more preparation than new ones – stripping old coats of paint and varnish, cleaning dirt and wax, and treating rusty metal – but, in the end, they will have a unique quality and charm.

Wooden chair
remove wax then varnish or paint

Wooden headboard
strip old varnish then varnish or paint

Metal watering can
treat rust then paint with metal paint

Wooden cupboard door
fill grain then varnish or paint

Old Objects

ABOVE AND RIGHT Old objects can provide some excellent shapes for decorating and are full of character. But they often need a lot of preparation.

Wooden door panel
remove wax then varnish or paint

Painted wooden door panel
strip paint then varnish or paint

To prepare plastics, especially those that are not too shiny, paint directly with paints that have a high chalk content. Glass requires no preparation other than thoroughly cleaning the surface to ensure that no smears are visible. New wood, especially pine with a number of knots, needs to be treated with shellac, a traditional varnish also used to prevent sap from seeping through the paint. Many new objects made of cardboard and particleboard are available for painted decoration and make a trouble-free base, although their mass production means that they lack character. Homemade or bought papier-mâché objects also provide a good base. Do not become too obsessed with preparation, however, or the search for a perfect surface may detract from the creative process of decoupage.

New Objects

BELOW AND RIGHT Many newly-bought objects can be decoupaged directly. However, some new surfaces may need a little preparation.

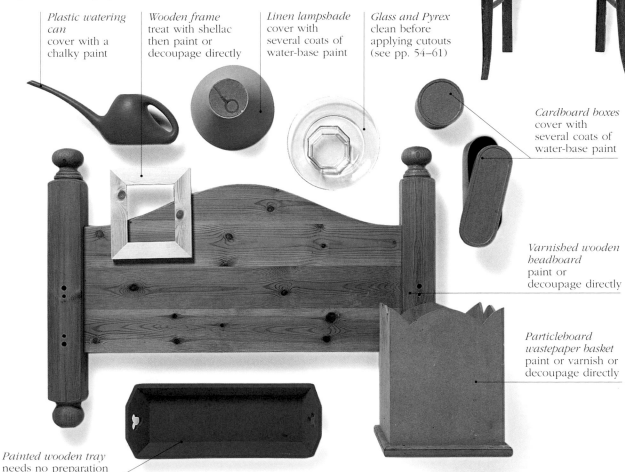

Varnished wooden chair paint or decoupage directly

Plastic watering can cover with a chalky paint

Wooden frame treat with shellac then paint or decoupage directly

Linen lampshade cover with several coats of water-base paint

Glass and Pyrex clean before applying cutouts (see pp. 54–61)

Cardboard boxes cover with several coats of water-base paint

Varnished wooden headboard paint or decoupage directly

Particleboard wastepaper basket paint or varnish or decoupage directly

Painted wooden tray needs no preparation

Backgrounds

A CUTOUT MOTIF CAN take on very different looks, depending on its background. The most basic background is a plain, painted one, which is what most people use when they begin. If the background is white, the effect is simple and useful as a base for alternative varnishing techniques (see pp. 40–47). A yellow crackle varnish, for instance, results in an antique ivory effect (see p. 45). Strong-colored pictures can withstand bolder backgrounds, perhaps picking up one of the colors in the cutout. Decoupage also looks highly effective against paint-effect backgrounds,

Plain Painted Background

BELOW *The zebra motif is on a plain, off-white-painted background. The white stripes of the zebra and the off-white back-ground echo one another. The back-ground of the round box (right) is a deep, classical red, providing great contrast to the motif.*

Paint-effect Background

ABOVE *The zebra motif is on a green, colorwashed background (bright green base and dark green glaze). The round box (right) has a frottaged background in deep red and two greens, which looks like marble and gives solidity to the design.*

such as ragging, frottage, or sponging. These give texture and depth to the background and you can keep the varnishing of them simple.

Wood is a more unusual background for a cutout, but it can look extremely effective, especially if it echoes the design in some way. Other unusual backgrounds are metal leaf, such as Dutch metal, copper, or aluminum (see pp. 66–69). You can also use metallic papers, although they are not as shiny as metal leaf. And there are many decorative patterned or abstract papers that you can use as the background to a cutout design. Wrap the paper over a piece of furniture or use it on a panel, with the main cutout motif on top. You may find that a busy decoupage design benefits from a plainer background, but experiment with different backgrounds to discover what brings your particular cutout to life.

Dutch Metal Leaf Background

BELOW The compass motif is against a background of Dutch metal leaf, an imitation gold, which gives an unusual, shiny effect.

Wood Background

BELOW The stripes of the zebra are echoed in the striped grain of the walnut wood. On the panel (right), the grain looks like running water, the sky, and the line of the river bank as well.

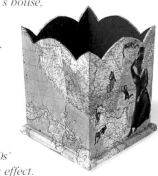

Paper Background

ABOVE The zebra motif is set against brick paper for a doll's house, creating a surreal effect. Leaves cut from wrapping paper occasionally overlap the zebra. The background of old maps on the wastepaper basket (right) gives the robust, rounded figures from the 1930s' paintings a dramatic effect.

Sources of Decoupage

Figure taken from an old gardening book and enlarged

T HE KEY TO CREATIVE decoupage is to have plenty of pictures available for cutting up. Traditionally black and white prints were used and then hand colored, but today there is a huge range of printed material. An excellent, inexpensive source is wrapping paper, but catalogs and good-quality magazines are also useful. Photocopy any copyright-free pictures that are too precious to use or are printed on thick paper. Sort your picture collection into themes, such as flowers, dogs, and china plates, and store them in separate boxes until you are ready to use them.

Book of architectural ornament

Black and White Pictures

LEFT AND BELOW There is a vast source of black and white prints including old books and catalogs. You can also buy specialty books of images suitable for decoupage. Either use them as they are, or photocopy them (see copyright note p. 15) to enlarge or reduce the size to meet the requirements of your project.

Book of Renaissance prints

Palm-tree print from an old children's encyclopedia

Book of decoupage designs printed on one side of the paper only

Old linoprint cards, found in a second-hand store

Diamond-shaped motif, original size and enlarged

Large paper print of swags and garlands for a print room

Print Room Pictures

RIGHT Borders and print room devices (see pp. 70–75), such as swags, ribbons, garlands, and chains are printed by specialty companies. They come on parchment-colored paper ready for cutting out. Use them on walls and furniture.

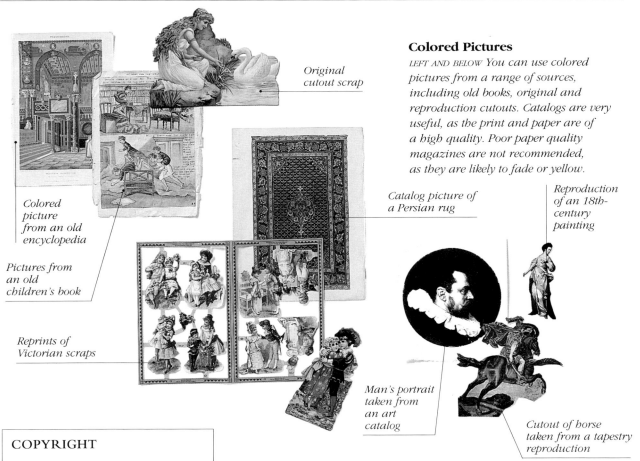

Colored Pictures

LEFT AND BELOW You can use colored pictures from a range of sources, including old books, original and reproduction cutouts. Catalogs are very useful, as the print and paper are of a high quality. Poor paper quality magazines are not recommended, as they are likely to fade or yellow.

Original cutout scrap

Colored picture from an old encyclopedia

Pictures from an old children's book

Reprints of Victorian scraps

Catalog picture of a Persian rug

Reproduction of an 18th-century painting

Man's portrait taken from an art catalog

Cutout of horse taken from a tapestry reproduction

COPYRIGHT

Although copyright laws may vary from country to country, you must not sell or photocopy an image that is under copyright to someone else, unless you have their written permission. Look carefully at a sheet of wrapping paper to see a printed note of who owns the copyright. Similarly you can find this information at the front of a book or magazine. Most publishers are happy to give permission, but they will charge you if your design is for commercial use. The templates at the back of this book are available for personal use. Some publishers produce books of black and white images specially intended to be reused without any copyright problems.

Colored Photocopies

BELOW You can get color photocopies made of pictures in books (see copyright note). It is especially useful to be able to enlarge or reduce a picture to the size you require. Over the years the color may fade, so try to apply a varnish that contains an ultraviolet filter.

Enlarged photocopy of painting taken from a book reproduction

Patterned Papers and Postcards

BELOW Wrapping paper (see copyright note p. 15) is readily available and comes in a vast range of designs. If you want to use wallpaper, look for ones that are not too thick. You may need to soak postcards in water or vinegar, to remove the thick card backing, before applying them (see p. 27).

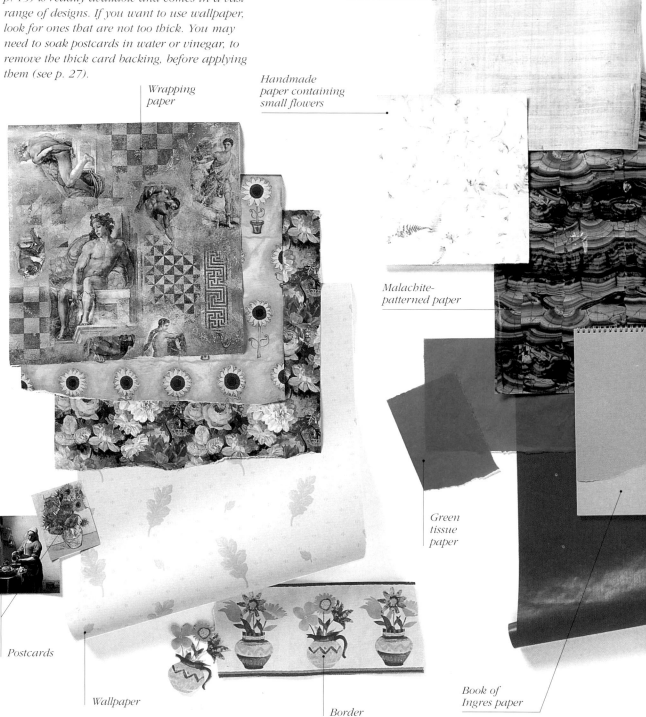

Papyrus

Wrapping paper

Handmade paper containing small flowers

Malachite-patterned paper

Green tissue paper

Postcards

Wallpaper

Border

Book of Ingres paper

Plain Papers

LEFT AND BELOW *Plain papers or papers with an overall repetitive abstract pattern are useful for creating your own motifs (see pp. 76–87). Buy them in the form of writing paper and wrapping paper, or from specialty paper shops or art stores.*

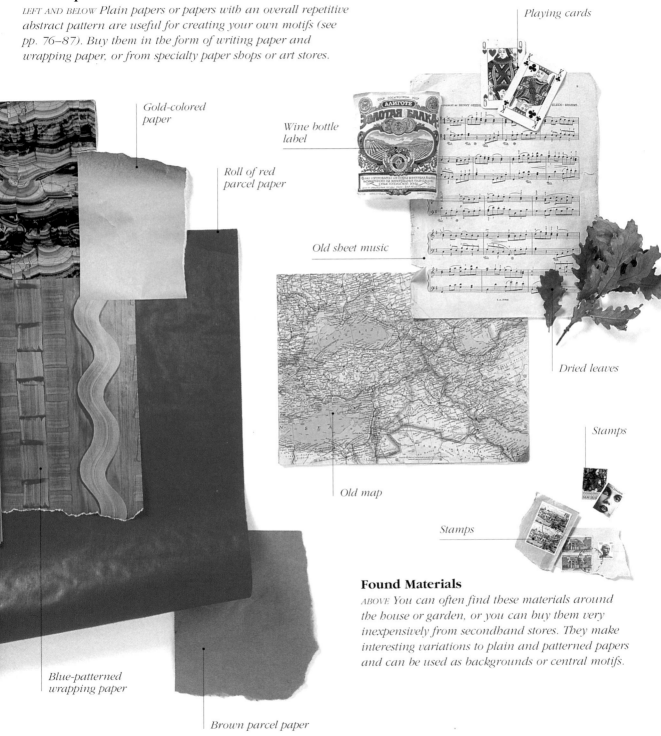

Playing cards

Gold-colored paper

Wine bottle label

Roll of red parcel paper

Old sheet music

Dried leaves

Old map

Stamps

Stamps

Blue-patterned wrapping paper

Brown parcel paper

Found Materials

ABOVE *You can often find these materials around the house or garden, or you can buy them very inexpensively from secondhand stores. They make interesting variations to plain and patterned papers and can be used as backgrounds or central motifs.*

Preparing Surfaces

Y OU CAN CREATE an elegant and sophisticated look with decoupage, provided that your surface is properly prepared. Even a small blemish or imperfection will show up if it has not been treated first. The tools and materials that are used to prepare surfaces (see pp. 20–21) are illustrated below. They are available at most hardware or art supply stores. When preparing surfaces you may want to invest in a pair of sturdy protective gloves that, as well as protecting the hands, allow you to heavily work a piece of furniture with steelwool or scrapers. Work in a well-ventilated room.

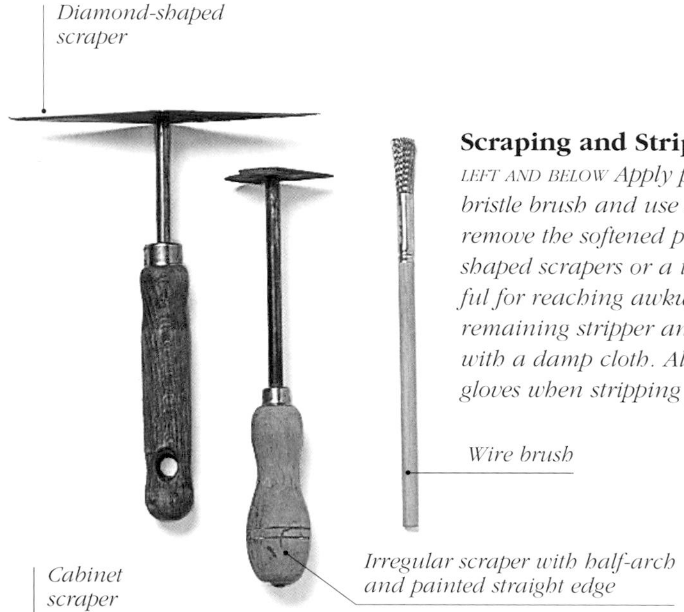

Diamond-shaped scraper

Scraping and Stripping

LEFT AND BELOW Apply paint stripper with a bristle brush and use steelwool and scrapers to remove the softened paint or varnish. Specialty shaped scrapers or a thin wire brush are useful for reaching awkward areas. Remove remaining stripper and loose paint particles with a damp cloth. Always wear protective gloves when stripping paint.

Soft cloth

Wire brush

Cabinet scraper

Irregular scraper with half-arch and painted straight edge

Heavy-duty protective gloves

Bristle brush

Steelwool

Scraper

Paint stripper

Filling Wood

RIGHT Use fillers on woods with holes or a pronounced grain, which may be visible even through several layers of paint. Remove loose dust after sanding (see Sanding and Painting below) with a damp sponge and use flexible scrapers to push the filler into the grain or hole.

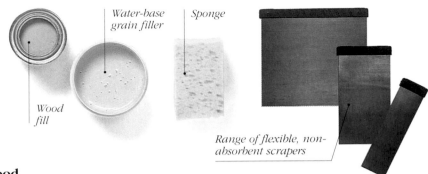

Water-base grain filler

Sponge

Wood fill

Range of flexible, non-absorbent scrapers

Removing Wax and Cleaning Wood

RIGHT Use a wax remover with steelwool and a soft cloth to clean your surface. Cover knots in new woods with shellac, a traditional varnish also used to prevent sap from seeping through to the paint surface. Clean your brush in denatured alcohol/ methylated spirits.

Denatured alcohol/ methylated spirits

Wax remover

Shellac and paintbrush

Fine steelwool

Soft cloth

Treating Rust

BELOW Use a wire brush to rub away existing loose rust and apply a rust inhibitor with a paintbrush. Use a paint specifically designed for use with metal.

Rust inhibitor

Bristle brush

Metal paint

Wire brush

Sanding and Painting

RIGHT Varying grades of sandpaper are useful throughout the process of preparing wood. Before painting use a tack cloth to pick up all the fine dust made while sanding.

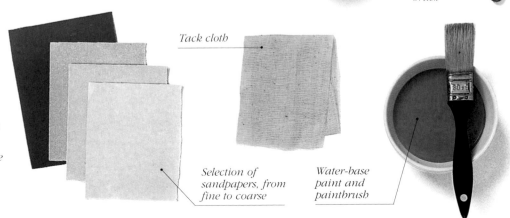

Tack cloth

Selection of sandpapers, from fine to coarse

Water-base paint and paintbrush

Using Paint Stripper

  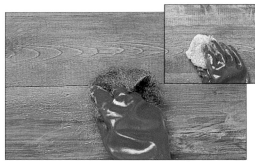

1 *Wearing protective gloves, apply paint stripper with a strong bristle brush. Wait until the paint or varnish begins bubbling (see manufacturer's instructions).*

2 *Keeping the scraper at a low angle to the surface, remove the bulk of unwanted paint or varnish. Apply a second coat of paint stripper if necessary.*

3 *Rub coarse steelwool all over the surface, then wipe with a damp cloth to remove any loose particles (inset).*

Removing Wax

  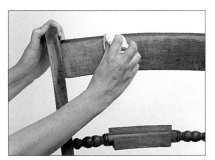

1 *Soak very fine steelwool in wax remover, then rub it over the surface. Wax remover dries in 5 minutes, so tackle a small section at a time. Do not allow the steelwool to dry out.*

2 *Using a wire brush, or a toothbrush, rub any carved or turned areas vigorously.*

3 *While the surface is still wet, remove old wax, dirt, and wax remover with a soft cloth.*

Filling Wood

1 *Rub the surface of the wood with fine sandpaper, working in the direction of the grain.*

2 *Wipe the surface with a damp sponge to remove the loose dust. Leave the surface damp, but not wet.*

3 *Using a non-absorbent scraper, work a water-base wood filler into the grain. After 20 minutes, rub with fine sandpaper as in Step 1.*

Treating Rusty Metal

1 Rub the metal with a wire brush to remove any loose and powdery fragments of rust.

2 Paint the surface with rust inhibitor, following the instructions for the brand you are using. Allow to dry.

3 If white marks appear, as here, rub the metal again with a wire brush and repeat Step 2.

4 Paint your object all over with a paint specifically designed for use on metal.

Preparing New Wood

1 Using a scraper, fill any holes made by knots with wood fill. Allow to dry for about 10 minutes, depending on the size of the holes.

2 Rub the wood using medium-grade sandpaper, working in the direction of the grain, to smooth the filled holes.

3 Using a paintbrush, apply clear shellac to the knots. Allow to dry for 5 minutes. Clean your brush in denatured alcohol/methylated spirits.

4 Using a paintbrush, paint the surface of the wood with water-base paint diluted with one-third water. Spread the paint evenly. Allow to dry.

5 Using medium-grade sandpaper, rub all over the surface, working in one direction only, so that you do not make any scratches. Remove the dust with a tack cloth.

6 Apply a second coat of undiluted paint, working in one direction only, so that no brushstrokes are visible. Spread the paint evenly. Allow to dry.

The Basic Techniques

TOOLS AND MATERIALS • 24

PREPARING MOTIFS • 26

STAINING AND COLORING • 30

GLUING • 36

VARNISHING AND FINISHING • 40

Tools and Materials

DECOUPAGE REQUIRES FEW tools, some of which you may already have at home. When you begin, improvize by using any available pair of scissors, glues, and brushes. When you are ready to give your work a professional look, you will need to invest in some quality materials, including a craft knife and blades, sharp pointed scissors, a variety of washable glues, drawing inks, water-base paints, and watersoluble pencils.

Cutting and Sealing Tools

RIGHT A large pair of sharp, pointed scissors is necessary for cutting out big areas. For delicate shapes, use small, sharp, pointed scissors such as sewing or embroidery scissors. A sharp, good-quality craft knife (with changeable blades) is ideal for cutting out intricate and awkward shapes. To seal your paper (see p. 27) before cutting out your motif, use water-base varnish and an acrylic varnish brush.

Sewing scissors

Water-base varnish

Acrylic varnish brush

Craft knife

Large pair of scissors

Embroidery scissors

Glues

RIGHT There are many suitable glues, but make sure you choose a glue that will not mark or leave a stain when you wipe away excess amounts. It must also be thin, so that it does not leave lumps under the paper. The glue should not dry too quickly after contact, since you may need time to adjust your design.

White glue

Starch glue

Gum glue

Flat-ended brush

Sponges, Cloths, Tweezers, and Rollers

BELOW AND RIGHT *Once you have glued your picture to the surface, you should remove the excess glue with a damp sponge or cloth. Sometimes you may need to use tweezers to pick up or replace small pieces of paper that shift when you wipe them. On large designs you can also use a roller to flatten the paper and dislodge any air that has become trapped.*

Soft cloth

Roller

Tweezers

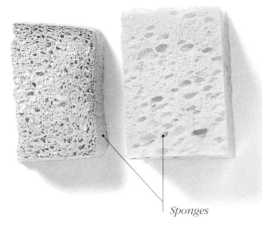

Sponges

Coloring Tools and Materials

LEFT AND BELOW *Black and white pictures can be lightly colored with drawing inks or any water-base paint. Oil-base paint is only suitable as a base to decoupage on glass (see pp. 54–61) or for painting freehand around paper motifs. You can use shellac or tea to age a black and white print or colored picture giving a light, yellowish-brown effect.*

Watercolor paints

Green ink

Green opaque water-base paint

Blue ink

Shellac

Watersoluble colored pencils

Fine artist's brush

Blue opaque water-base paint

Teabag

Preparing Motifs

THE METHOD OF PREPARING your decoupage motif depends on the nature of the design and the object you intend to apply it to. If you are using a photocopy, the paper may be thin and delicate and the inks likely to spread, so it is a good idea to seal the image with water-base varnish before you cut it out. If the image you want is on a postcard you will need to remove the card backing first. Most people prefer to use scissors for straightforward cutting, but for fine, intricate details it is often easier and looks neater to use a craft knife. Try to create a fluid, soft line, since any angular edges will look unnatural. Think carefully about how you cut a design if you are going to apply it to a round object (see p. 28).

Small Scissors

RIGHT A pair of small, sharp scissors would be a good choice here because the man and horse design is broad and not too detailed.

Small scissors

Broad design

Craft Knife

RIGHT Use a craft knife when cutting shapes as intricate as these flowers, especially around the petals.

Craft knife

Intricate design

Border

Postcard

Large Scissors

RIGHT To cut long straight lines use either a craft knife or a pair of large scissors. Small scissors would result in a curving, uneven line.

Large scissors

Postcard

ABOVE To prepare a motif from a postcard, remove the thick card backing by soaking it in vinegar.

Sealing the Motif

If your paper is particularly thin or delicate and likely to tear easily, or the picture surface is fragile and likely to rub off while you are gluing it down, sealing with water-base varnish is a good idea. Test a small area of the picture first to ensure that the inks do not run when you apply the varnish. Use an acrylic varnish brush to apply a single coat of water-base varnish to your picture. Do not overload your brush or apply the varnish too thickly, since the paper may crinkle if it becomes too wet. Allow the varnish to dry completely, for at least 10 minutes.

Peeling a Picture off Heavy Card

Some pictures, such as postcards, are too thick to use directly for decoupage, as they require too many coats of varnish to be practical. But postcard pictures are often a good source of decoupage subjects if you remove the card backing, leaving a thin picture, which you can then cut and use.

1 Using a piece of cotton, apply ordinary white vinegar to the back of a postcard until it begins to soften.

2 Starting at the corner, along one edge, peel away the backing. Work patiently, continually applying more vinegar.

3 The wetter the backing becomes, the easier it is to remove. Rub it gently and pieces will roll or pull off easily (right). Allow the very thin picture (far right) to dry naturally before cutting and using.

Using Scissors

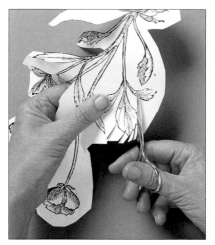

1 Cut off the excess paper surrounding your motif. Here, a picture from a book of flower prints was photocopied (see copyright note p. 15) and enlarged.

2 Holding your scissors hand still, make snips into the design along lines that face in the same general direction. Move the paper to accommodate small changes of direction.

3 Turn the paper slightly, then cut in the opposite direction, across the snips you have already made. The excess paper will fall away, and the leaf will begin to take shape.

4 You can reach central areas by cutting between parts of the design – here, between the stem and the leaf.

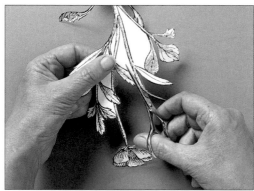

PITFALLS

If you do not carefully follow the outline of your picture, you will end up with visible white edges, as here around the knees, arms, and feet. These will show up even on a white background. Change your cutting tool to see if this makes it easier.

5 Alternatively, poke the scissors into the central area and cut toward the edges. Take great care when doing this since the position of your scissors may be awkward, causing you to cut off or break delicate outer shapes.

Using a Craft Knife

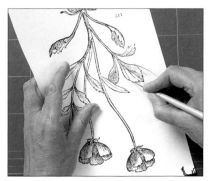

1 Place the picture on a cutting board. First, make cuts into the design along lines facing in one direction, turning the paper slightly as necessary.

2 Next cut carefully around the shape, working close to the lines but leaving them just visible. Keep the knife in one place while you move the paper.

3 Then cut out central areas, such as those between the stem and leaves in this picture. Tackle delicate parts, such as the stem, last, so that they do not get broken off.

Cutting a Picture for a Round Object

If you have a round object, and a motif that winds all around the object, you will probably need to cut the motif into separate sections and overlap it, in order to make it fit smoothly against the curve. You can hide the places where you have cut the design by cutting along existing lines.

1 Place the design around your object and look to see where you may be able to cut it. Here, the border can be cut approximately every 2in/5cm to fit it around the bowl.

2 Cut along existing lines in the design – here, where the leaves curl to one side about halfway into the design. It is better to make too many cuts than too few.

3 When you glue the design to your round object, overlap the cut edges, making sure that a foreground part of the design overlaps a background part. The end result should be that none of the cuts look obvious.

Staining and Coloring

A BLACK AND WHITE MOTIF can be embellished by staining or coloring. Tea stains paper to give it an aged look whereas watercolor paints, inks, and watersoluble pencils are easy to use and can give your motif a subtle or a bright effect. Use a mix of shellac and pigment to give your motif a three-dimensional quality or fill in the background of your motif in a color that matches the base color of the object being decoupaged. Generally, do your coloring before cutting out your motif. That way it does not matter if you go over the edges. However, for painting in highlights and backgrounds it is best to cut and glue first.

Tea

BELOW *Photocopies are printed on bright, white paper. Stain them with tea to dull the brightness.*

Photocopy

Strong tea and teabag

Pigment and Paint

RIGHT AND BELOW *Embellish classic motifs with subtle highlights and shadows using shellac, pigments, and paints.*

Pigment

Paint

Shellac

Modern motif

Ink

Inks

RIGHT *The bright clarity of inks gives an old-fashioned look to a modern motif.*

Ink

Watercolor paint

Classic motif

Busy design

Paint-brush

Traditional motif

Watersoluble pencils

Watercolor Paint

ABOVE AND RIGHT *Watercolor paints are light and transparent, suitable for subtly coloring traditional motifs.*

Watersoluble Pencils

ABOVE *Gently color an already busy design with watersoluble pencils.*

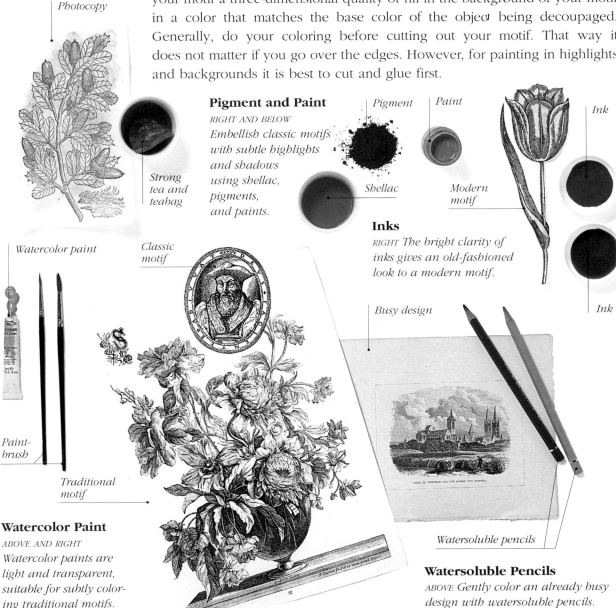

Staining Large Motifs with Tea

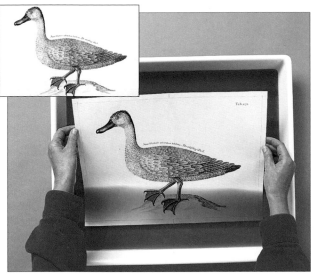

1 *Make a tray of tea large enough to dip your picture in without crumpling it. Use a strong tea solution of four teabags steeped in 1pt/600ml water for 20 minutes. Dip the whole motif, sliding it from one side to the other to avoid tidemarks. Leave for a few minutes until soaked.*

2 *Remove the picture and place flat on newspaper. Dab, not wipe, the picture with a dry, clean cotton cloth to remove excess water. Leave the motif to dry naturally, without putting it near excessive heat.*

Staining Small Motifs with Teabags

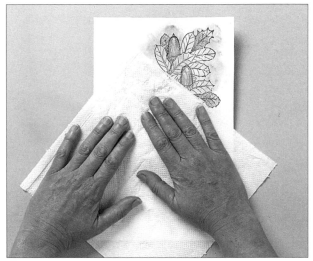

1 *Dab your motif all over with a damp, but not dripping wet, teabag to release color from the tea leaves. To keep the color from looking too uniform, squeeze out more tea in some areas for darker color and less in other areas for lighter color.*

2 *Soak up the excess tea with a tissue, to prevent the paper from becoming waterlogged and crinkled. Allow the motif to dry naturally, without putting it near excessive heat.*

Coloring with Watercolor Paints

Watercolor paints, available either in tubes or in cakes from art supply stores, are the traditional way of coloring black and white motifs. Test the colors on scraps of paper before using them, so that you know their strength. Be careful not to waterlog the paper, or it will crinkle.

1 Wet the cake of paint and transfer a small amount on your brush to a mixing tray. Dilute the color with water to at least half its original strength. Test on some scrap paper. Here, two colors were mixed together.

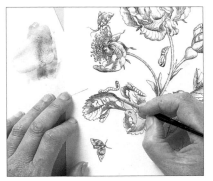

2 Apply paint, starting in the cross-hatched (shadow) areas, making these darker, and get lighter as you move out. Err on the side of lightness, as the color will often dry darker and you can always add more color later.

3 Add darker colors, here green-brown, to the flower, again starting in the cross-hatched areas and getting lighter as you move out. Do not over complicate the design with too many colors.

Coloring with Inks

1 Apply the ink with a soft artist's brush, working speedily, because the ink soaks in and dries quickly. Mix inks to obtain the exact color you want, or dilute them with water for a lighter tone.

2 The inks give bright, clear colors. Paint them on roughly to imitate early color printing, where colors were often misaligned. When you cut out the motif it will look sharper.

Coloring with Watersoluble Pencils

Using colored pencils that are soluble in water is an easy way to color black and white prints. Simply shade a small area where the color needs to be strongest and, with a wet artist's brush, spread the color onto the rest of the area that you want to color with that hue.

1 Start with the lightest colors, and use the colored pencil to shade in areas you want in that color. Scribble lightly with the pencil, leaving gaps between patches of color.

2 Use a stronger, darker red on the shadow areas of the flower heads, where there is cross-hatching. Add hints of green in the other cross-hatched areas.

3 On other parts of the design – here, the base of the butterfly's wings – add a hint of brighter color to add interest.

4 Dip an artist's brush in a little water and brush the pencil color into other areas. Let some areas remain pale while others have concentrated puddles of color.

PITFALLS

If you add color too brightly and too thickly, as with the yellow on these daffodils, some of the design will be obliterated. Also, because the color was added after the design was glued down, the result is messy.

5 To increase the darkness of the shadows and to add depth, use more dark red. You can either leave this as it is, or wet it with the artist's brush, but do not spread the color. If in doubt, add a little color at a time. You can always build up a greater depth by repeating the process.

Painting in Shadows and Highlights

You can give a black and white motif a three-dimensional aspect by hand painting shadows and highlights. Although this looks impressively difficult, it is merely a matter of following the original design. Try not to fill in the whole drawing, but to give dashes of color that will catch the light.

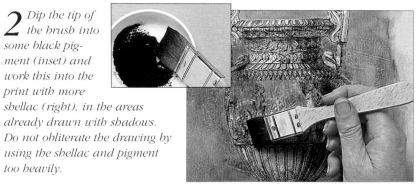

2 Dip the tip of the brush into some black pigment (inset) and work this into the print with more shellac (right), in the areas already drawn with shadows. Do not obliterate the drawing by using the shellac and pigment too heavily.

1 After sealing (see p. 27) and gluing (see pp. 36–39) your motif to the surface, apply a coat of dark shellac ("button polish" or "garnet polish"), using a soft-haired, flat-ended brush. Let dry for 20 minutes.

3 Using a fine artist's brush, apply beige water-base paint to parts of the drawing that are not in shadow. Add some white to the lightest areas in a few places, to enhance the three-dimensional effect.

4 The print of the urn is transformed into something of great dramatic quality.

Painting in the Background

1 Here, an intricate pastoral scene was glued (see pp. 36–39) to a base covered in blue water-base paint. Seal the base and picture with water-base varnish (see p. 27) to prevent the paper from being absorbent.

2 Resting your hand on a piece of paper to avoid spoiling the work, paint in the background of the picture. Use the same blue that you used for the base. Reach into delicate parts of the design, such as the leaves of the trees, using a fine artist's brush.

3 Varnish the picture to seal it and give it the same tone as your sealed base (inset). Your painted background may look mottled (below) or more solid, if you apply a second coat.

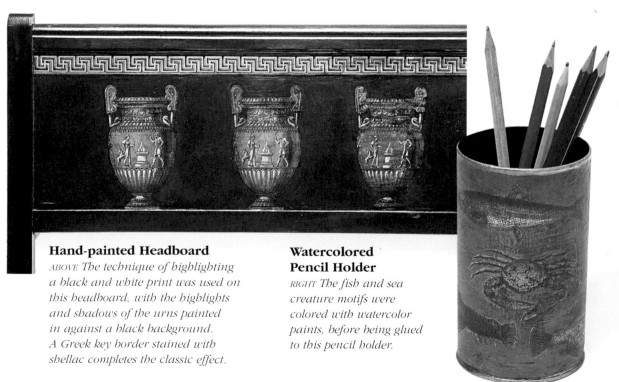

Hand-painted Headboard

ABOVE *The technique of highlighting a black and white print was used on this headboard, with the highlights and shadows of the urns painted in against a black background. A Greek key border stained with shellac completes the classic effect.*

Watercolored Pencil Holder

RIGHT *The fish and sea creature motifs were colored with watercolor paints, before being glued to this pencil holder.*

Gluing

G LUING IS A SIMPLE process, but if you do it without due care it can create unsightly curled edges, folds, and bubbles. The general rule when gluing is to apply the glue to the surface, rather than to the paper – particularly with delicate pieces – to prevent damaging the design, or saturating the paper, which makes it lose its shape. It is also important to take care when removing excess glue from around your motif and removing air bubbles from underneath the motif, which can be done using a damp sponge, or, for large designs, a roller. Gum-base glues and starch glues are used predominantly in this book, but white glue is equally suitable. When using glue, work in a well-ventilated room.

White Glue

BELOW White glue (also known as PVA) is a strong glue often used for sticking wood together. It is a good glue for using with thick paper.

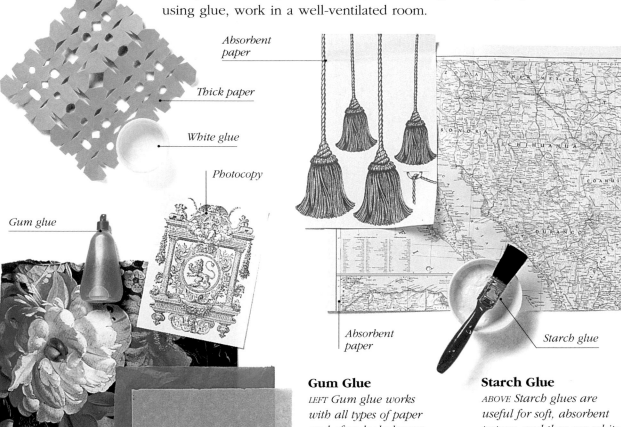

Absorbent paper

Thick paper

White glue

Photocopy

Gum glue

Absorbent paper

Starch glue

Wrapping paper

Tissue paper

Gum Glue

LEFT Gum glue works with all types of paper and often looks brown. It gives you enough time to move your design around but, once dry, the paper adheres permanently.

Starch Glue

ABOVE Starch glues are useful for soft, absorbent papers, and they are white in appearance. They enable you to reposition the paper. Once the glue is dry you can dampen the motif to remove it.

The Basic Technique

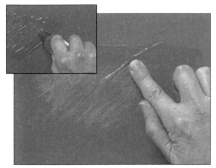

2 Holding your motif in both hands, place it carefully in position. Begin with one side and smooth it down, working across to the other side to help stop air bubbles forming.

1 Apply glue to a varnished or painted surface (inset), spreading it with your finger to ensure an even covering.

3 Working from the center out toward the edges, wipe the design gently with a damp sponge or cloth to remove any air bubbles and glue trapped underneath.

4 Dab all excess glue from the area surrounding the motif with the damp sponge. Wash out the sponge and repeat. Excess glue can prevent varnish from adhering.

5 Pay particular attention to the edges of the design, pressing them down with your fingers. This will help remove any excess glue from underneath and ensure that the corners are firmly in place.

PITFALLS

To avoid creating folds in your motif make sure the sponge is not too wet. Wipe gently just a few times with the sponge and then dab the surface, so that the paper stretches evenly.

Gluing Delicate Work

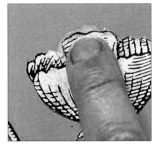

1 Apply glue to the surface as in Step 1 of The Basic Technique *(see p. 37). Here, the roots of the flower, the thickest part of the motif, were used to position the motif and were glued down first. Move gradually outward, gluing the next part of the design.*

2 Use tweezers to lift delicate parts of the design. These allow you to reposition a piece already glued, without tearing the paper.

3 Press down with your fingers all over the design, to remove excess glue and ensure that no parts remain unglued.

4 Dab the design with a damp sponge. Do not wipe with it, except very gently, because it is too easy to tear the delicate pieces.

5 Rewet the paper so that the fibers soften and the motif becomes flexible and easy to shape. Make use of the stretchiness of the paper, particularly with these long, thin flower stalks by making the flower heads point in different directions. This gives an individual quality to the work, particularly if you repeat the design several times. Once the paper is dry, you can remove any excess glue by wiping with a sponge.

PITFALLS

Take care to remove all the glue from around the edge of your motif, or the excess glue will get dirty. For the same reason, be sure to use a clean sponge to remove glue.

Using a Roller for Large Areas

Some people like to use a
roller to flatten down a
large motif while it is still
wet. Roll from the center
out and apply a lot of
pressure. Do this before
any bubbles form in
the paper, or you may
make creases.

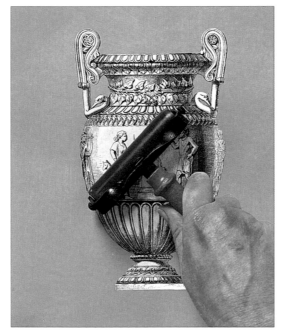

White Glue-covered Frame

BELOW White glue was used with
heavy brown paper to cover this
frame. The glue was also used
as a varnish.

Starch-glued Print

ABOVE Because starch glue was used
to position this print, you could
reposition it later, if necessary. No
varnish was applied, so although the
print is perfectly secure, you could
take it off the wall with care, by
dampening gently with water.

Gum-glued Box

RIGHT A simple gum glue was applied to the
lid of this box, allowing sufficient time to
place the print in the exact position required.

Varnishing and Finishing

THE AIM IN VARNISHING your decoupage is to be able to pass your hand over the design and not feel the paper. This is why upward of 10 coats of varnish are often necessary, depending on the thickness of the paper and the type of varnish you use. At this stage you can also add decorative touches to your decoupaged objects by coloring the varnish, using crackle varnish, or scratching varnish for an aged effect.

There are two kinds of varnish to consider. Modern varnishes, such as water-base varnishes and specialty decoupage varnishes, dry clear and quickly (see manufacturer's instructions); decoupage varnish needs only 5 or 6 coats. Traditional varnishes, such as oil-base varnish, specialty aging varnish, and shellac, dry with a yellowish-brown tinge for an aged effect. Be sure to work in a well-ventilated room.

Modern Varnish and Pigments

RIGHT Use water-base varnish (also known as acrylic varnish) on its own to give a clear, unobtrusive effect. There are flat and glossy types, although the glossy or satin varnish is the strongest. Apply with an acrylic varnish brush for the best results and spread gently. You can use pigments to color the varnish. Each pigment has a different strength – some are very strong and a little goes a long way. It is best to be cautious, tinting the varnish slightly so that you do not obliterate the motifs.

Red oxide pigment, very powerful

Prussian blue pigment, powerful and bright

Oxide of chromium, powerful and becomes opaque easily

Water-base varnish and acrylic varnish brush

Raw umber pigment, not very strong

Crackle varnish

Cloth for applying oil-base paint to cracks

Oil-base paint

Aging varnish

Strong-haired flat-ended brush

Shellac

Oil-base varnish

Soft-haired flat-ended brush

Traditional Varnishes

LEFT AND ABOVE *Use these varnishes to give your decoupaged object a yellow tinge for an aged effect. Oil-base varnish dries very slowly. If you like the quality of oil-base varnish, it is possible to use water-base varnish first and then finish off with an oil-base one. Shellac (sometimes known as "French," "button," or "garnish polish") is based on denatured alcohol/ methylated spirits, and dries extremely quickly to give a high gloss to your work. Aging varnish combined with crackle varnish and some oil-base paint will give a distinctly antique look to your work.*

Scratching Varnish

BELOW AND RIGHT *Scratching water-base varnish with steelwool is another way of imparting an antique look, and helps to give color and patina to the motif.*

Cotton cloth for wiping clean

Dark green-blue water-base paint

Coarse steelwool

Firm-bristled brush

Dark red water-base paint

Sponge for wiping off excess paint

Applying Varnish

Here, the three basic varnishes are
used to cover three similar motifs,
enabling you to see the different kind
of finish they provide, and the right
brush to use with each to give your
work a professional quality.

Water-base Varnish

RIGHT Use an acrylic varnish brush,
which is soft but strong enough to
push the varnish over the motifs
without leaving brushmarks. Try not
to overbrush, which will cause
streaking marks. Apply 10 coats of
water-base varnish or 5 coats of
specialty decoupage varnish.

Oil-base Varnish

ABOVE If you apply oil-base varnish directly to paper,
you may get a patchy appearance. Avoid this by first
applying a coat of water-base varnish. Oil-base varnish
gives the appearance of age by removing the stark white-
ness of the paper. Use a strong-haired flat-ended brush
and apply 15 coats.

Shellac

ABOVE Here, the clearest, least colored shellac is being
used. Other shellacs known as "button polish," "garnet
polish," and "French polish," have more brownish or
yellowish tones. Do not overbrush, because shellac dries
very quickly and you may cause streaking. Use a
soft-haired, flat-ended brush and apply 7–8 coats.

Mixing Pigments into Varnish

1 Apply a layer of water-base varnish all over your motif. You can do this step after applying several layers of varnish or at the first coat, so that you apply more varnish on top.

2 Dip just the corner tip of your brush into the pigment (inset), since you need only a little to stain the motif. Work the pigment into the still-wet varnish. You may require extra varnish in order to work the pigment in.

3 Work a second or third color into the first one. Here, red oxide is being added and mixed with Prussian blue and raw umber. Work quickly.

4 Fill in the background of your motif with other colors – here, green with raw umber. This picture was covered with water-base varnish (right), but you could use oil-base varnish or shellac.

Scratching Varnish

1 Apply at least two coats of water-base varnish to your motif and allow to dry thoroughly for three hours or more, or the varnish will peel off when scratched.

2 Using very coarse steelwool, scratch the surface of the varnish. Try to avoid circular motions, which look unnatural. Scratch in straight lines in all directions, sometimes with long strokes, sometimes with short ones.

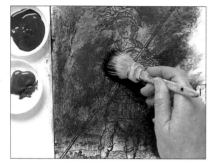

3 Using a water-base flat paint, work a firm-bristled brush into the scratchmarks. Use dark-colored paints, such as the greenish-blue and reddish-brown ones used here.

4 Before the paint is dry wipe it off with a damp sponge. The paint will remain in the scratches (right).

Crackle Varnish

1 To make a crackle effect you need two varnishes (an oil-base one and a crackle varnish). Here, oil-base aging varnish is being applied over a motif. You can use a standard oil-base varnish instead. The motif was first sealed with water-base varnish.

2 When the oil-base varnish is partly dry, apply the crackle varnish. If it does not adhere, the oil-base varnish is still too wet. The drier the oil-base varnish, the smaller the cracks will be.

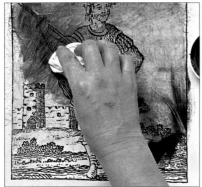

3 The cracks will appear as the crackle varnish dries. Use a hair dryer gently to speed up the process. When dry, rub a dark oil-base paint into the cracks and wipe off any excess with a soft cloth.

4 The finished result gives fine cracks all over the surface (inset), helping to give the picture an antique look. By using ordinary oil-base varnish instead of aging varnish, you get a less brown effect. Cover with a final coat of oil-base varnish for protection.

Pigment and Varnish Lampshade

RIGHT Raw umber pigment was used with a water-base varnish over the flowers and landscapes on this lampshade. This helped to harmonize the prints, some of which are brighter than others.

Scratched-varnish Tray

BELOW The scratched-varnish technique was used on this tray. Black water-base paint was brushed into the scratches over the motif and the terra-cotta paintwork. It was then varnished again, using a water-base varnish.

Shellac-covered Box

LEFT Dark shellac was applied over the Dutch metal leaf on this red box. This gave it a high lacquer shine and deepened the whole effect.

Scratched-varnish Panel

ABOVE This black and white print was lightly colored using watercolor paint (see p. 32), covered several times with water-base varnish, then scratched with coarse steelwool. A dark-colored water-base paint was then brushed into the scratches.

Crackle-varnished Frieze

RIGHT This frieze shelf, or mantelpiece, of decorative jugs, bowls, glasses, and tankards was crackle varnished to bring the design together, although some areas were left bare to highlight the aged effect. Larger patches of dark oil-base paint give the uneven look.

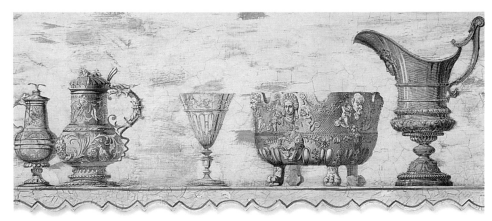

Pigment and Varnish Letter Rack

LEFT This red and green painted letter rack was covered with water-base varnish. Red and green pigments were then worked into the still-wet varnish to create this effect.

Water-base Varnished Frame

BELOW To preserve the strong contrast and clarity of the black and white prints on this frame a specialty decoupage varnish was used to quickly give a high gloss.

Crackle-varnished Boxes

BELOW The ivory effect of the two boxes was achieved using a crackle varnish over an oil-base varnish. Dark brown oil-base paint was rubbed into the cracks.

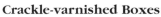

Applying the Techniques

Traditional Decoupage

Traditional Headboard

A collection of portrait paintings creates the theme for this headboard. The young girl at the top provides the focus, with the two adults directly underneath giving support. The overlapping background comprises pictures of fabrics, carpets, and landscape paintings.

DECOUPAGE IS OFTEN closely associated with the traditional 18th century technique of entirely covering a surface by scrupulously overlapping cutouts. At the start of the 20th century artists had adapted this technique to make collages by combining printed pictures, plain paper, fabrics, and three-dimensional objects. Today, precisely positioning motifs is no longer considered important, unless the designs are detailed. The trick to working with detailed cutouts is to set them on the surface, trace the elements to mark their positions, then use the tracing paper to realign your motifs when gluing them down. To ensure the success of any decoupage project, take the time to plan your composition before gluing in place.

TOOLS & MATERIALS

Masking tape for positioning design

Border for scrap design

Landscape for collage

Reproduction scraps and other pictures

Glue

Sponge

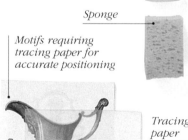

Motifs requiring tracing paper for accurate positioning

Tracing paper

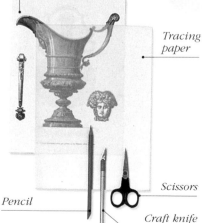

Pencil

Scissors

Craft knife

The Basic Technique

1 Release some Victorian-style scraps from their border or cut out some colored pictures, but not in great detail; simply let each scrap form one solid piece of paper.

2 Divide your scraps into large, medium, and small designs – large background pictures, and smaller, focal pictures. Make a loose arrangement of them.

3 Glue down the large background motifs first (see pp. 36–39). Position the medium-sized scraps over the edges of these scenes. Try to visualize where the main picture will go.

4 Now add small scraps, such as butterflies, flowers, or fans. You can cover the whole background or let small areas of background paint show through.

5 To make a neat edge, use a border strip that you bevel, or slant, at the corners. The border should cover any straggling scraps. Cut away any overhanging strips with a craft knife.

6 The main picture gives a focal point to the design but does not dominate it. The five butterflies provide a secondary, unifying theme.

Precise Positioning Using Tracing Paper

1 Cut out a selection of photocopies (see copyright note p. 15) very carefully, then arrange them in place on your background.

2 Lightly tack down the individual designs with small pieces of mounting putty or tacky tape, to prevent the designs from moving.

3 Fix tracing paper or waxed paper over the design with mounting putty. Trace the design to mark the position of the different elements.

4 Remove a couple of photocopies at a time, and glue them in place (see pp. 36–39). Check their position by realigning the traced design.

5 Remove the tracing paper and wipe off excess glue with a sponge. Varnish (see pp. 40–47).

Making Collage Pictures

1 Gather together a collection of pictures, including one large main picture to use as the background. This could be a landscape, a street scene, or even a house interior.

2 Cut an incision into the main picture. Here, the fish will slot into the background so that it appears to emerge from it.

3 Enhance the three-dimensional look by placing one motif behind another – here, the hare behind one tulip stem and in front of the other.

4 So that the motifs do not overlap the edge of your main design, draw a pencil line down the edge and then cut off any overlaps.

5 Glue all the motifs in position (see pp. 36–39), wiping off any excess glue with a sponge (inset). This scene has a surreal effect because cutouts of varying proportions were used.

Precisely Positioned Cupboard Panel

RIGHT *The inner panel of this cupboard was made to look like shelves containing vases, plates, and jugs. Paper borders were pasted on to imitate the shelves, then the objects were arranged with the help of tracing paper.*

Overlapping Trunk

ABOVE *This chest was decorated with overlapping sea creatures and chains against a mottled green background.*

Collage Tray

RIGHT *Figures and landscapes from old master paintings were cut out of an old diary and overlapped on this tray to make a landscape collage.*

Decoupage on Glass

Decoupaged Glass Bowl

Medieval scenes were cut out and glued on the inside of this glass bowl. Deep terra-cotta was then painted over the cutouts to make the figures and background appear as one. This simple yet highly effective technique created the look of an antique hand-painted bowl. The inside of the bowl was varnished for protection.

DECORATING GLASS using paper offers many possibilities. The basic method of glass decoupage is to glue your cutout motifs to the back of the glass, so that you view the scene from the front through the glass. You can either apply opaque oil-base paint over the back so that no light can filter through, or use the light itself; shapes, such as flowers or trees, cut from tissue or other delicate paper can create a translucent effect. A crackle paint background allows the light to show through and an arrangement of colored, translucent papers creates a stained-glass effect. Black silhouettes on window panes, with no painted background, provide a dramatic look. Alternatively, glue a design to the outside of a glass bowl so you can view it from the inside. The permutations are almost endless. Apply glass decoupage to great effect on bowls, goblets, plates, windows, cabinets, and doors.

TOOLS & MATERIALS

Paper motif

Glue

Oil-base paint

Sponge

Paintbrush

Crackle medium and brush for applying it

Water-base paint

Black paper for silhouettes

Transfer metal leaf

Water-base gold size and brush for applying it

Fine artist's brush

Colored tissue paper

The Basic Technique

1 Place the cutout paper motif (see pp. 26–29) on the glass pane to determine where you want to position it, either in a central position or slightly further down the glass.

2 Move the motif to one side and apply a thin, even layer of glue (see pp. 36–39) to the back of the pane (the reverse side from which you will view the design).

3 Place the motif, picture side down, on the glass, moving it carefully into position while the glue is still wet. Take care, as thin pieces of the motif can easily break.

4 Turn the glass over to check that the motif is correctly positioned. Look for any air bubbles, which are more obvious when you are viewing the design through the glass.

5 When dry, wipe off all excess glue with a damp sponge (inset). Apply two coats of oil-base paint all over the back of the glass, covering the motif. The finished design shows through the glass (right).

Applying Decoupage to the Outside of a Bowl

You can apply decoupage to the outside of a glass bowl, so that you view the decoration from the inside. In this way you can use the bowl for food.

Varnish the bowl (see p. 42) to make it washable. Use very thin paper, such as the wrapping paper used here, which you can cover easily with paint.

1 Turn the bowl upside down and apply a coat of glue to the surface (see pp. 36–39).

2 Stick the motifs upside down to the base and sides of the still-upturned bowl. Use a damp sponge to remove excess glue.

3 Paint the base and sides of the bowl with oil-base paint. Here, enamel paint was used, which is a strong paint available from craft stores.

4 The stars are viewed through the bowl for an individual effect. You can also use vehicle spray paint to great effect for this technique.

Using Crackle Paint

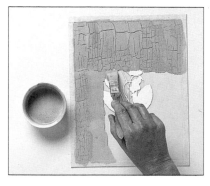

1 Glue your cutout motif upside down to the back of the glass (see pp. 36–39) and allow to dry. Using a soft, flat-ended brush, paint crackle medium all over the back of the glass. Allow to dry for at least 20 minutes.

2 Apply a water-base paint quickly and without interruption. Make sure there is enough paint on your brush for each brush-stroke. Do not overlap the brushstrokes after the paint has begun to dry or you will pull the paint off.

3 The finished effect, when viewed through the glass, gives a textured background, which contrasts well with the delicacy of the flower design.

Silhouettes on Glass

Silhouettes in black or colors, such as dark blue or green, look highly effective behind glass. You can take designs from books of silhouettes, adapt them from stencil designs, or draw round pictures. The traditional silhouette is the profile of a face, but birds, animals, leaves, and flowers also work well.

1 Photocopy (see copyright note p. 15) and enlarge, if necessary, a silhouette design. Place a piece of tracing paper on top and, using a light-colored crayon or pencil, trace the outline of your silhouette.

2 Reverse the tracing paper and place it on black paper or another dark color. Retrace the line you have already drawn.

3 Cut out the silhouette using a pair of sharp scissors. Remove the crayon or pencil marks by cutting just inside the line.

4 Apply a thin, even layer of glue (see pp. 36–39) to the back of the glass. If the paper is absorbent, you may need to wet it slightly before gluing it to avoid a patchy effect.

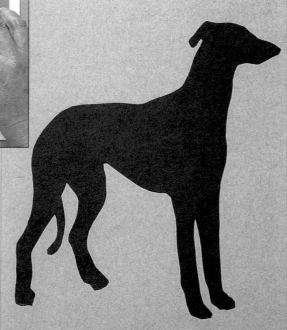

5 Press the paper silhouette down in the required position. Wipe over it with a damp sponge (inset) to remove any air bubbles. Viewed from the front the silhouette on glass has a dramatic effect.

Using Metal Leaf on Glass

The effect of metal leaf behind a picture, seen through glass, can be stunning. The glass acts like a high-quality, smooth varnish, giving extra sheen to the metal leaf. Metal leaf, here Dutch transfer metal leaf, an imitation gold, is adhered with a special glue called gold size (see pp. 66–69).

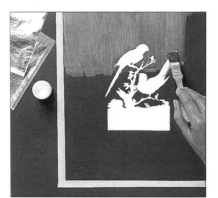 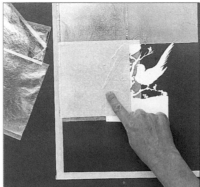 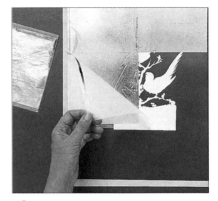

1 Glue your motif (see pp. 36–39) upside down to the back of the glass. With a soft, flat-ended brush, apply water-base gold size all over the glass. Leave for 10 minutes until no white color is visible.

2 One piece at a time, position the transfer leaf over the gold-sized glass, holding it by the overhanging waxed paper. Slightly overlap the preceding sheets. Press down the leaf by rubbing over the waxed paper.

3 Remove the waxed paper, working gradually over the whole area. If any gaps or tears appear, take some more metal leaf and restick it. Apply a little more gold size if it will not adhere.

4 Using a large, soft gilder's mop (see p. 67) or similar soft brush, wipe away any excess metal leaf. Wipe the leaf again, particularly around the picture edge, with your fingers or with the mop brush to ensure close contact between the metal leaf and the motif.

5 The colors of the motif work well against the gold background and the metal leaf gives attractive definition to the design. The effect changes in different lights. Varnish the back (see p. 42) to protect it from tarnishing.

Stained-glass Effect

1 Take a stained-glass design from a book of such designs or from a drawing or enlarged photocopy (see copyright note p. 15). Place it under the glass.

2 Place colored tissue paper over the front of the glass and secure with masking tape. Trace on the tissue paper the shapes you want in that color. You may also find it useful to secure the design under the glass with masking tape.

3 Cut out the tissue paper shapes and place them on the design. Repeat Steps 2–3 using different colored tissue paper for different parts of the design.

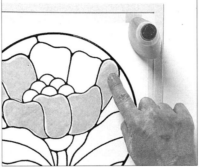

4 Place glue on a small area on the back of the glass. Dab the tissue paper down with your finger.

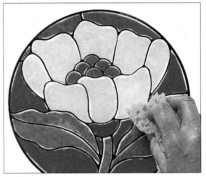

5 Because tissue paper is fragile when wet and tears easily, dab rather than wipe the paper with a damp sponge to remove any excess glue.

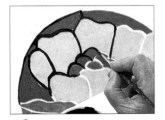

6 Using an oil-base paint, and a fine artist's brush, paint a black line around each paper shape.

7 With the light behind, the design looks bright and its colors come to life.

PITFALLS
Take care when dabbing tissue paper with a damp sponge, to ensure that it does not tear and the dye does not spread to other parts of the design.

Sheep Bowl

ABOVE AND LEFT A naïve-style sheep from a greeting card was glued inside this bowl. Dutch metal leaf was applied behind it, leaving small gaps in which green, black, and white water-base paints were applied.

Silhouette Plate

ABOVE Silhouettes of country animals and birds were glued to the back of this glass plate. It was then sprayed with bright red paint to create a strong contrast with the dark animal shapes.

Stained-glass Door

ABOVE AND RIGHT The panels of this glass door were given a stained-glass effect, inspired by medieval stained-glass windows.

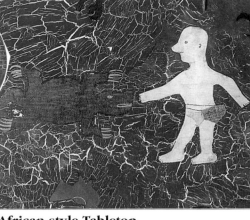

African-style Tabletop

LEFT AND ABOVE This glass tabletop uses paper cutouts of people, animals, fish, and birds taken from appliquéd African designs. The background is blue crackle paint sealed with shellac, which is then painted white to give definition to the cracks.

Oriental Vase

LEFT Two Chinese-style paintings of birds were cut from an art magazine and glued to the inside of this vase. A strong green oil-base paint with a little brown was then sprayed on top of the paintings.

Silhouette Lantern

LEFT The silhouette design on this lantern was first sprayed with adhesive spray, then pressed into position on the glass.

Leaf Bucket

RIGHT Leaves taken from a wallpaper design were glued inside this glass ice bucket. It was then sprayed with black vehicle paint.

Decoupage with Freehand Painting

H AND PAINTING A SURFACE to create a loosely textured background is a good way to give your decoupage designs an authentic historical look. This approach particularly suits 18th-century scenes, where landscapes often have a slightly blurred look, with more defined painting of people and animals in the foreground. For extra decorative effect you can add in stylized painted clumps of grass or even shadows around the cutout decoupage. You could also adapt the technique to make seascapes and watercolor-style backgrounds (see p. 65). Alternatively, hand painting details on tissue paper decoupage gives a unique, three-dimensional quality.

Hand-painted Chest of Drawers

This chest of drawers was decorated with scenes from 18th-century rural paintings collected from auction-house catalogs. Some of the cutouts were cut in two, to allow for the gap between the two drawers. Grass and shadows were painted on to anchor the images to the background and prevent them from looking as though they are floating.

TOOLS & MATERIALS

Blue water-base paint

Small paintbrush

Off-white water-base paint

Large paintbrush

Dark green water-base paint

Light blue water-base paint

Terra-cotta water-base paint

Paper motifs

Sponge

Glue

Water-base varnish and acrylic varnish brush

Water-base paints

Colored tissue paper

Artist's brush

The Basic Technique

1 Apply blue paint to the top half of the surface. While the paint is still wet work in some white (inset) to create contrasts between pale blue and dark blue areas. Apply the paint unevenly. Be careful not to overbrush.

2 Apply dark green paint, starting at the base of the picture area and working up to meet the sky area in the center. Use white to merge the horizon line, where the green and blue meet (inset).

3 You can add brighter colors in a few places to lift the background. Here a few streaks of bright blue were added to the sky and terra-cotta was added to the ground. Allow to dry for about 5 minutes.

4 Cover the paint with a water-base varnish (either medium-sheen or glossy) to prevent the glue from sinking into the water-base paint when it is applied. Allow to dry thoroughly, which will take about 15 minutes.

5 Position your paper motifs (see pp. 26–29) on the painted background and glue them down (see pp. 36–39) when you are happy with the arrangement.

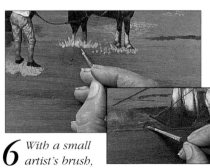

6 With a small artist's brush, add thin vertical lines to simulate grass and dark horizontal lines (with softened edges) to simulate shadows (inset). Apply varnish (see pp. 40–47).

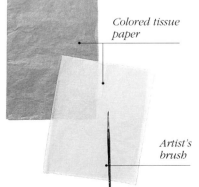

Freehand Painting on Tissue Paper

1 Draw a design of flowers, leaves, or other simple silhouette shapes. Intricate shapes do not work well with fine tissue paper.

2 Transfer your design to different colored sheets of tissue paper, using colors appropriate to your design, either by drawing it again or by tracing it carefully.

3 Cut out the tissue paper design with sharp scissors (inset). Cut out all the pieces before starting to glue them.

4 Tear the flower petals out of tissue paper, to give them a soft edge. Use white tissue paper for the flower centers. Glue the flowers into position.

5 Allow the design to dry for 3–4 hours. It will look messy now, but the design will come to life at the next stage.

6 Using water-base paint and a fine artist's brush, paint circles, spots, lines, and outlines on the flowers and leaves.

7 Here, the bowl was outlined in white, as if the light was coming from the left. The right side was outlined in a darker color, and a smudge of deep blue was rubbed on the side of the bowl to give it depth. Apply several coats of water-base varnish (see p. 42) for protection.

(see p. 42)

8 The translucent nature of the tissue allows you to "see" through the foliage and flowers, giving the design a three-dimensional quality.

Classical Box

ABOVE: Hand-painted pearls were added around the edge of this frottaged and decoupaged box.

Persian-style Box

LEFT AND BELOW Photocopied Persian paintings were arranged on a background of pale blues, greens, and mauve. Small tufts of grass and flowers were hand painted between the horsemen, and lines around the box lid.

Leaf and Berry Curtain Pole

ABOVE AND LEFT Strips of tissue paper were glued around this curtain pole. The berries were painted with dark shadows and highlights to give them shape, and the leaves with a central vein for definition.

Fish Tray

ABOVE AND RIGHT Black and white pictures of fish were glued to this dark blue and black tray. Lines and dots of color in blue and off-white water-base paint were added in between to create a stylized water effect.

Decoupage with Metal Leaf

METAL LEAF IN GOLD or Dutch metal (imitation gold leaf), silver, and copper gives tremendous richness to your work and lends it an exotic quality, whether you use it as a background to decoupage, or on the motifs themselves. Metal leaf is available in both loose and transfer forms (leaf that has been pressed onto waxed tissue paper for easier handling) and is used with a special glue called gold size, which does not tarnish the leaf. You can gain inspiration from designs taken from the past. For example, Persian miniature painting often uses a background of gold for delicately painted pictures of horsemen and beautifully robed people. Asian lacquerwork uses gold designs against a background of strong, positive colors, such as bright red, black, olive green, or terra-cotta.

Decoupage on Metal Leaf Lampbase

ABOVE The loose Dutch metal leaf on this lamp-base makes a powerful background to the shield-shaped heraldic picture glued on top.

Decoupage with Metal Leaf Bureau

RIGHT This small bureau was decorated in the style of 18th-century lacquer-work. Asian figures and animals cut out of paper covered with Dutch metal leaf were glued onto a black painted background. A coat of shellac gave the bureau a glossy finish.

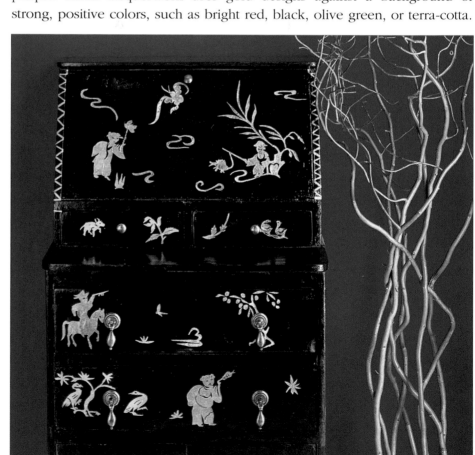

TOOLS & MATERIALS

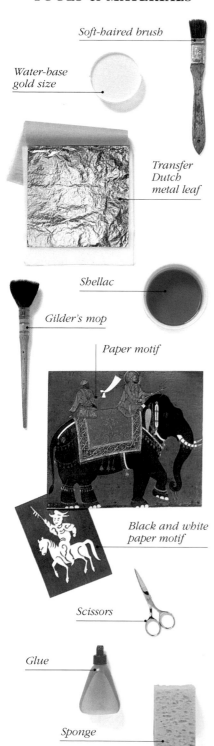

Soft-haired brush

Water-base gold size

Transfer Dutch metal leaf

Shellac

Gilder's mop

Paper motif

Black and white paper motif

Scissors

Glue

Sponge

The Basic Technique

1 Using a soft-haired brush, apply a coat of water-base gold size to a painted background and leave for 5–10 minutes, until it becomes sticky. The size will remain tacky indefinitely.

2 Apply sheets of transfer metal leaf to the size. Overlap each square until you cover the whole area.

3 With a gilder's mop, wipe off any excess metal leaf. If any areas remain uncovered, try to restick the metal leaf to them.

4 Varnish the entire area with a coat of shellac to protect it from the glue (see pp. 40–47), and let dry for 10–15 minutes. Or, use an oil-base varnish, and let dry for 1 to 2 days.

5 Apply glue to the metal leaf over a slightly larger area than your motif and fix your motif in place (see pp. 36–39).

6 Using a damp sponge, smooth down the motif and remove all excess glue.

Metal Leaf on Motifs

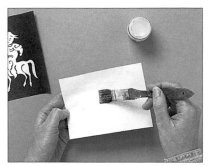

1 Using a soft-haired brush, apply a coat of water-base gold size to the back of a silhouette-style motif. Allow to dry for 5–10 minutes. The gold size will remain tacky indefinitely.

2 Apply the transfer metal leaf to the tacky picture back. The leaf will adhere immediately. Press it down with a gilder's mop or a dabbing motion of your fingers.

3 Cut out the design with sharp scissors, using the silhouette on the front as a guideline. Do not discard the small pieces that you cut away. You can use them to make smaller motifs in your final design.

4 To protect the metal leaf, varnish all over the shiny side with shellac, or with a slower-drying, oil-base varnish (see p. 42).

5 Glue your design onto your background (see pp. 36–39). Choose a background color that forms a strong contrast with the metal leaf, such as the deep red used here.

Dutch Metal Standard Lamp

ABOVE This floor lamp was covered in loose Dutch metal leaf. Pictures of flowers taken from French textile designs were then glued to the surface. It was varnished with shellac for protection.

Metal Leaf Portraits

BELOW These portraits were given an exotic look by positioning them against a metal leaf background. The dark colors of the two heads stand out against the copper and Dutch metal leaf, while the full-length portrait is offset by the background pattern of spirals and triangles.

An Elizabethan figure and black cutouts against aluminum metal leaf

Copper Leaf Frame

ABOVE This red painted frame was decorated with paper covered in copper metal leaf, cut into birds, leaves, and spiral-shaped tendrils. The shapes were left slightly in relief after three coats of varnish, in imitation of lacquerwork.

A woman's head against distressed Dutch metal leaf

A man's head against copper leaf

The Print Room

THE TRADITION OF print rooms began in 18th-century Great Britain. Etchings or engravings were glued to the wall and complemented by borders, swags, ribbons, and garlands. The print room loosely copies the traditional arrangement of real paintings and the rococo fashion of stucco decoration on the wall. Try to use original black and white prints, rather than photocopies, and buy accessories, such as borders, ribbons, and swags from specialty stores. Before embarking it is essential to find a group of prints that work together, perhaps on a theme such as ancient Greece, plants, or birds. Alternatively, you can adapt the method to a single print, framed and pasted on a wall or small object.

The Print Room
This entire room was decorated with prints and borders. The tasselled ropes were glued in different positions, adding a lively elegance. A frieze was added to the top of the wall around the room.

TOOLS & MATERIALS

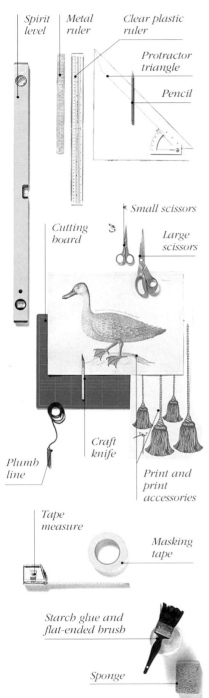

Spirit level

Metal ruler

Clear plastic ruler

Protractor triangle

Pencil

Small scissors

Cutting board

Large scissors

Plumb line

Craft knife

Print and print accessories

Tape measure

Masking tape

Starch glue and flat-ended brush

Sponge

Preparing a Print

1 *Using a large protractor triangle or a T-square, draw a pencil line around the print, making certain the corners are right angles – old prints are often not straight. Here, equal space was left on all sides of the single, central motif. Be careful not to get finger-prints on the print, which will show up later.*

2 *Draw a second frame, about ¼ in/6mm outside the first. You can do this with an ordinary ruler, but it is easier with a clear plastic ruler – align one of the ruler lines with your inner pencil frame and draw another pencil line downward.*

3 *Find the central point of each line by measuring it, and make small pencil marks. Do not mark the print inside the inner frame.*

4 *Cut along the outer pencil line on all sides of the print, using large, sharp scissors or a craft knife. To give your print an aged look at this stage, stain it with tea (see p. 31). Prepare all the prints in the same way before proceeding to the next step.*

Framing a Print

1 Place small pieces of masking tape all round the underside edge of the print, so that the sticky side of the tape is uppermost.

2 Choose the border design for your print. Cut sufficiently long lengths of border so that it overlaps at each corner. Secure the border to the masking tape, aligning it with the inner pencil line.

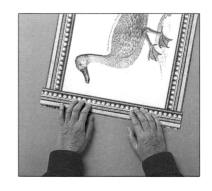

3 Place a metal ruler diagonally from corner to corner of the overlapping borders. Using a craft knife with a sharp blade, cut along the ruler. Don't worry if you cut through to the print.

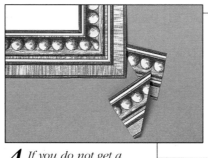

4 If you do not get a good corner match (inset), you can hide it, using corner tabs (right).

Adding the Framework

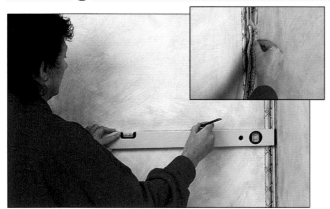

1 Piece together border strips in the corner of the room, until you have covered the full height of the wall (inset). Using a spirit level at right angles to the corner strips, draw a pencil line along it at the correct height for the chair rail.

2 Apply glue to the back of the paper chair rail. Using the pencil line as a guide, press the paper chair rail onto the wall across the entire room.

3 Within the area below the chair rail, mark out panels in pencil. Cut out and glue down border strips to delineate the panels.

Measuring

1 Using small pieces of masking tape lightly fix the prints in position on the wall. Adjust them until you are satisfied with the grouping. Lightly tack down ribbons, ropes, swags, and other details. Mark the top center of each print lightly in pencil on the wall.

2 Remove each print one by one and use a plumb line – a weight attached to string and used to determine verticality – to accurately mark their central positions on the wall.

Finishing

1 Remove the border strips and immerse the print in a tray of cold water for a minute or so (inset). Remove and place upside down on spare paper for gluing. With a flat-ended brush, apply a generous coat of starch glue.

2 Position the print on the wall, aligning the central mark on the print with the central mark on the wall. Use a plumb line to make sure that the line is vertical. Dab with a damp sponge to flatten the print.

3 Glue ribbons, swags, and other details in position, and add the border frames. Although print rooms are not traditionally varnished, you can add one or two coats of varnish for protection (see p. 42).

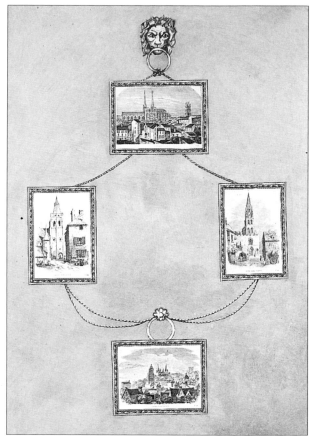

Print Room Walls

ABOVE AND RIGHT An old print of palm trees was combined with floral swags and a central architectural device hung with flowers (above). Prints of French villages were brought together using ropes, against a toning beige background (above right). A rich, deep green paint picked up the greens in these botanical prints, while the traditional print room borders helped to harmonize the colors and unify the group (right).

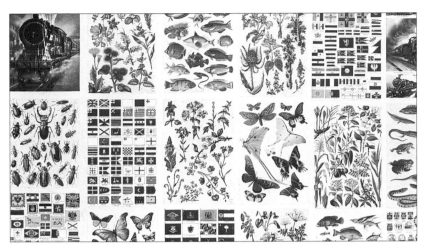

Continental-style Print Room

LEFT These prints from an old children's encyclopedia have varied themes, but work well together. They were cut to regular sizes and pasted close together.

Two Wastepaper Baskets

RIGHT AND BELOW The black wastepaper basket has a central motif and complementary borders. The cream wastebasket was decorated with borders and swags, and then crackle varnished (see p. 45).

Key Box

ABOVE A homemade 1930s' hand-printed woodcut found in a secondhand store was used on this small key box. The strips were cut from classical borders to match the dark main motif.

Garlanded Hat Box

RIGHT This hat box uses decorative devices that are traditionally used between the images of a print room, as well as borders. It has a lining of marbled paper.

Classical Box

ABOVE This small round box with its circular border has a classical print taken from an old book as its central motif.

Making Your Own Designs

Stencil Motif Container

A Victorian-style stencil was used as a template for the motif on the front of this dried flower container. It was cut out of marbled paper and glued to a frottaged background in terra-cotta and green.

You CAN USE PLAIN and patterned papers to make your own designs, either freehand or with a template. Use a stencil as a template, or draw around a photograph to make a simple silhouette. Cut around a single motif on concertina folded paper to make a repeat pattern in a border. You can simply create your own designs in paper by cutting geometrical shapes out of folded paper, to reveal diamonds, triangles, and stars when you unfold it. Achieve a symmetrical motif by cutting half a design into a single folded sheet of paper, or create a completely individual effect by cutting circles, spirals, and slots into a solid motif. Keep your cut shapes simple and you can achieve some delightful results with which to decorate boxes, panels, drawer fronts, and lampshades.

TOOLS & MATERIALS

Wrapping paper

Stencil

Scissors

Craft knife

Pencil

Silhouette photograph

Tracing paper

Masking tape

Light-colored pencil

Black paper

Wrapping paper

Sponge

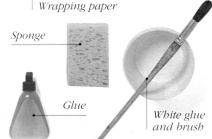

Glue

White glue and brush

Using a Stencil

1 Place your stencil design on your paper. Draw around the outside of the stencil card with a pencil. Here, a simple stencil design was used with wrapping paper.

2 Following your pencil marks, cut out the card shape. Because the paper has an abstract repeating pattern you can repeat the motif any number of times.

3 Place the wrapping paper on top of the stencil card and turn both card and paper over.

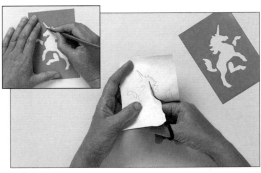

4 The white side of the paper will now show through the stencil shape. Draw around the stencil shape (inset), then cut it out (above).

5 To help position the design correctly, draw around the stencil shape on the surface where you want to glue it. Apply glue to the surface inside the pencil marks (see pp. 36–39).

6 Press the paper pieces into position (inset). In the final design (above) the two unicorns were placed facing each other.

Silhouettes

1 Silhouettes can come from a wide variety of sources, including the examples shown here: a book of traditional silhouettes (some of them are very complicated), a bird book, black and white drawings, a children's cutout, a colored picture, a leaf, and a photograph of someone in profile.

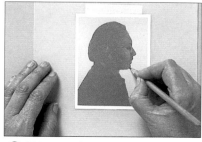

2 Using masking tape, secure some tracing paper over your silhouette. Trace the outline of your silhouette, using a very sharp pencil.

3 Turn the tracing paper over and draw over the traced line using a light-colored pencil that shows up against the black paper.

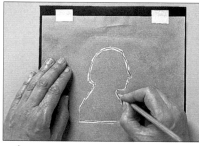

4 Turn the tracing paper over again and secure it to a piece of black paper with masking tape. Using a sharp pencil, trace over the design one more time.

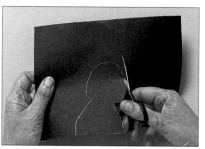

5 The light colored pencil marks will transfer to the black paper. Cut out the silhouette, following the light colored pencil lines.

6 Use this silhouette for any decoupage project. Here, the stark black paper cutout is on a colorful patterned background that lifts the design.

Folding Paper to Make a Repeat Border

1 Draw a design with a solid center and narrow extensions on each side – the trunk and tail of the elephant – to link the border. Draw a rectangle around the motif so that on either side the lines touch the narrow extensions of the motif. Cut out the rectangle to use as a template.

2 Cut a strip of patterned wrapping paper. Position your template on the back of the strip at a far edge. Mark in pencil the edge of the template. Position the template next to the first mark and mark again. Repeat until you have the desired amount of repeats. Fold the paper along these lines into a concertina shape.

3 Cut out the drawing and place on top of the folded paper strip. Trace around it. Make certain that the trunk and tail extend to the edges of the paper so that they will link the border.

4 Hold the folded paper strip in one hand and, with your other hand, cut through all the layers at once following your outline. The trunk and tail touch the edge of the concertina strip so you do not snip into them and they hold the border together.

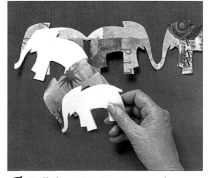

5 Pull the strip open to reveal a row of elephants holding trunks and touching tails. This asymmetrical design results in pairs of elephants, facing each other and back-to-back.

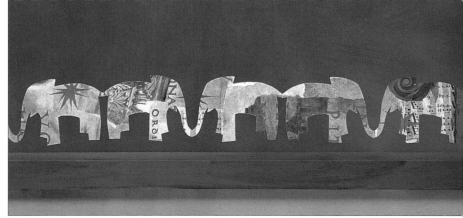

6 Glue the border (see pp. 36–39) to a strong-colored background. The random patterns and colors of the wrapping paper add interest to the design and break up the solid shape of the elephants.

Making a Geometric Design

1 Fold your paper – here, handmade paper, but you can use any paper – in half, and in half again. Fold it in half one more time. You can do more folds if your paper allows.

2 Cut notches along all four edges of the paper. Alter the length and width of the notches to give variety to the design.

3 Open the paper out once. This will reveal that there are areas of the paper where there are no holes.

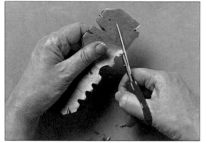

4 Fold the paper in the opposite direction from the direction you have just unfolded – here, lengthways – and cut more notches, altering the length and width, along the new fold.

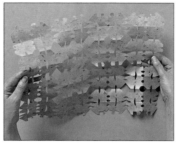

5 Unfold the paper fully to make sure you have cut into all the areas. You can make an enormous range of patterns.

6 Glue the cutout to your surface (see pp. 36–39). You can use any type of glue. Here, white glue was used.

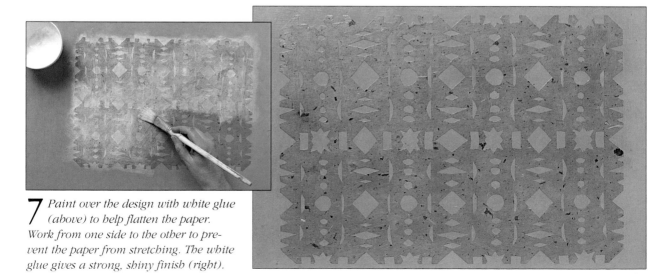

7 Paint over the design with white glue (above) to help flatten the paper. Work from one side to the other to prevent the paper from stretching. The white glue gives a strong, shiny finish (right).

Scissorwork

1 The red fish and the green dancing figures shown here are examples of Chinese scissorwork designs. The black and white bird design comes from Poland and the design with the figures and flag from America. These traditional ways of cutting paper to make designs might be inspiration for your own projects.

2 Draw a simple symmetrical image, such as the plant here. Draw a line down the center of your picture. Lay a piece of tracing paper over your drawing and trace the right half of the design.

3 Turn over the tracing paper and transfer the half design to colored paper by retracing over it, so that the original pencil line shows up.

4 Fold the colored paper in half along the edge of the design. Cut out the design, using sharp scissors and following the pencil lines.

5 Unfold the cutout, to get a symmetrical design. Glue to your background (see pp. 36–39).

Cutting Shapes

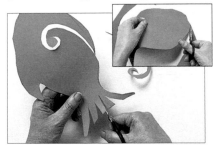

1 Draw a simple fish shape on colored paper, then cut it out with a pair of scissors (inset). Cut into the design from the edge to make spirals and a fringed edge for the tail.

2 Using a craft knife, carefully cut out slots and circles within the solid body of the fish.

3 This fish comprises simple cutout shapes. Starting with broad, basic designs and gradually cutting more intricate shapes is good practice for more complicated designs.

Symmetrical-patterned Cupboard

LEFT AND BELOW The panels of this cupboard were decorated with symmetrical designs that were made by cutting plain and decorative wrapping paper along a fold.

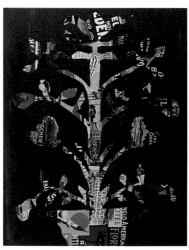

Silhouette Box

BELOW AND RIGHT Inspired by ancient Greek pottery, this silhouette of a profile was cut from black paper set against the orange lid of this box.

Stencil Motif Box

BELOW A stencil of a horse was used as a template here. The pieces were cut out of carpet designs taken from magazines and glued to this box.

Repeat-patterned Chest of Drawers

LEFT AND BELOW Folded and cut borders, based alternately on birds and flowers, were used on the drawers of this blue and green chest.

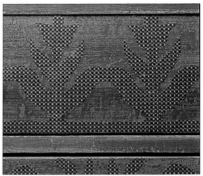

Silhouette Mirror

ABOVE Silhouettes of leaves from different trees were cut from black paper and glued against a background of wrapping paper that also has a leafy pattern to cover the frame of this mirror.

Geometrical Tabletop

RIGHT This wood tabletop was decorated with paper folded and cut into geometrical and other abstract shapes that were glued to patterned wrapping papers.

Building Designs with Colored Papers

Marble-style Chest

Gold, red, and malachite-patterned wrapping paper was used with paper from a catalog from a marble company to make panels, birds, flowers, and leaf shapes on this chest.

Y OU CAN USE A COMBINATION of plain or patterned papers to build up your decoupage design. Use torn, plain colored papers to create a simple, multi-colored motif with soft, lacy edges. You can also use wood-effect papers (available from specialty paper stores) against a wood background for an effect similar to ancient marquetry techniques. Use the same technique to imitate inlaid marble work, or to make a design that resembles an appliqué quilt.

TOOLS & MATERIALS

Plain papers

Plain paper

White glue and brush

Glue

Sponge

Papers with wood grain effects

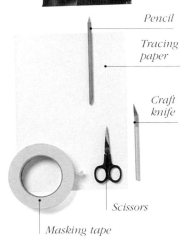

Pencil

Tracing paper

Craft knife

Scissors

Masking tape

Torn Paper Design

1 Draw a simple picture of a bird, using very basic shapes. Redraw different parts of the design onto different colored papers.

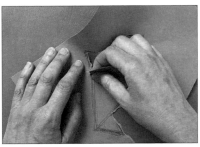

2 Tear the paper, following the lines as closely as possible. Tear all the parts out, holding the paper down with your other hand.

3 Turn the paper over so that the pencil lines are not visible. Assemble the picture, which now faces the other way.

4 Position the design correctly on some scrap paper. This will act as your guide when you start to glue the pieces down.

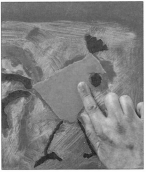

5 Brush white glue all over the background. Working from the guide, transfer all the pieces to the glued background. Press down with your finger, particularly around the edges.

6 Varnish all over the design, using either ordinary varnish (see pp. 40–47) or white glue (inset) to give it a strong, glossy finish.

Faux Marquetry

1 Draw a design – here, taken from an old marquetry clock front – that will work using three tones of wood-effect paper.

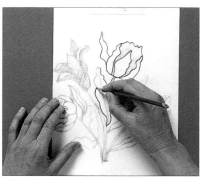

2 Trace the outline of the drawing onto tracing paper, keeping the shapes simple but delicate.

3 Assign a number to each shape corresponding to each paper – (1) the light paper, (2) reddish paper, and (3) the dark paper.

4 Turn the tracing paper over on scrap paper and scribble lightly all over the lines using a pencil or some pigment.

5 Turn the paper over again and position it on the light paper. Firmly retrace with a pencil over the shapes numbered for that color. Do the same for each shape.

6 On a cutting board, cut the shapes out of the paper using a craft knife (see p. 29). Cut out all the pieces for each color.

7 Retrace the design in the correct position on the wooden surface that you wish to decorate. Make sure the pencil line is visible against the wood.

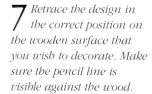

8 Glue the shapes in position (see pp. 36–39), using the numbered tracing and pencil lines on the wood as a guide. Wipe off any excess with a damp sponge.

10 *The finished effect, seen against the warm, yellowish wood, is a simplified version of part of the original 17th-century marquetry on the clock.*

9 *To give an extra dimension to your work, let the grain of the overlapping leaf shapes run in a different direction (above). To avoid having to join pieces accurately on the tulip, glue smaller, light-colored shapes over the darker shape (inset).*

Faux Marquetry Chair

LEFT AND BELOW A musical motif cut out of two kinds of wood-effect paper decorates this wooden chair back.

Appliqué-inspired Bedside Cabinet

RIGHT Flowery wrapping paper was used like scrap fabrics to decorate this bedside cupboard. The design is reminiscent of early American appliqué quilts.

Decoupage Library

Y OU CAN USE these images for any of the decoupage techniques featured in this book. Photocopy them at the same size, or reduce or enlarge them, and prepare the motifs by sealing, coloring, cutting, gluing, and varnishing (see pp. 26–47). The images are grouped by subject, with birds, animals, and fish on these two pages, flowers, plants, and fruit on pages 90–91, and borders and classical decorations on pages 92–93.

Birds, Animals, and Fish

Flowers, Plants, and Fruit

Borders and Classical Decorations

Index

How to Find Supplies

The tools and materials you need for the techniques demonstrated in this book are generally available from hardware stores, paint supply, or art supply stores. To find a store near you, try looking in your local telephone directory under paint, craft supplies, decorative materials, or decorator's supplies. If you are on the Internet, you can look there under the same categories, or you can try specialty magazines on crafts and interior decoration, where many of the stores and suppliers place advertisements. If there are no stores in your neighborhood, don't despair, as many of them have mail order facilities and you can send for a catalog.

You can also visit Annie Sloan's Internet site – *www.anniesloan.co.uk* – for further information.

Acknowledgments

Many thanks for the superb support I received from those around me, particularly David and, of course, the boys, Henry, Felix, and Hugo. Claire Waite, Mandy Greenfield, and Colin Ziegler did a brilliant job of marshalling my ideas and encouraging me along the way, for which I am very grateful.

Photographer Geoff Dann, his assistant Gavin Durrant, designer Steve Wooster, and Sampson Lloyd also deserve many thanks.

I would like to thank Nicola Wingate-Saul of Nicola Wingate-Saul Print Rooms (43 Moreton Street, London, SW1V 2NY Tel: 0171 821 1577), who gave me immense help and expert advice on the *Print Room* pages. She also provided the wastepaper baskets and hat box on page 75, the trunk on pages 1 and 53, and the prints on page 14. I am also extremely grateful to Joanna Casey (Mawley House, Quenington, Cirencester, Glos. G17 5BH Tel: 01285 750267) for providing the beautiful boxes on pages 39 and 47.

The paper used on the front and back cover is Merevale wallpaper, copyright Laura Ashley, 1995.

I used my own range of paints, varnishes, and glazes, which are available through Relics of Witney mail order (35 Bridge Street, Witney, Oxon, OX8 6DA Tel: 01993 704611).

Thanks also to the team at Relics of Witney, Bret Wiles, Chris Walker, and Ray Russell.